Advance Praise for
Get Top Ranking on Google & Other Search Engines

"I think a book like that is much needed in the small business community. You wouldn't believe the number of times I've had to rescue a website from being held hostage by an unscrupulous web designer....all because the business owner didn't know what questions to ask."

Paige Eissinger, Web Designer – Podcast Host
www.2smartchix.com
www.viewsfromthecoop.com

"This book needs to be read by every Independent Retailer who has any web presence whatsoever. It is a simple to follow, easy to understand book on how to make changes to your current site so that more customers can find you. I have read many search engine optimization articles and I thought that I was pretty good at optimizing my web site, but Greg taught me quite a few very valuable methods to help my visibility. Get this book, read it and then do it!"

James E. Dion, Internationally Renown Retail Consultant – Keynote Speaker www.dionco.com

"I really enjoyed reading your book...wow, I learned a lot! Your book reads somewhere between a 'SEO for idiots' and a typical how to; this is good. Easy to read and relate to in the first person....seemed like we were having coffee and talking. Great job Greg."

Sonia St. James, Consultant to Creative Minds, Author.
www.accelerprocess.com

"Greg I am impressed with your book. For sure you've captured your market if I am any indication. I know a lot about small business and almost nothing about the world wide web and optimizing my business through my website. As of now my site is still unfinished. I knew I was going to make rather drastic changes to it (we've changed our approach to the new cookie mixes and added new components that are now unrepresented on the site) but with the info I've learned through your book I'll be making changes that strategically optimize my chances of people finding me."

Penny McConnell, Bakery Owner – Small Business Advocate www.pennyspastries.com

"Greg has written his SEO book with down-to-earth language that everyone can understand. I found it incredibly relevant, useful, and even entertaining. My company will get a lot of use out of this book. As we are an online company, it is imperative that we have access to tools of this caliber. Greg has nailed it with this one."

Jeffrey Lorien, President/CEO – zhitea.com Austin, TX

"Greg thanks to your book I'm excited about my website again. I was reading it and suddenly I was making some changes on my web catalog, calling to the host company and taking notes. The term Search Engine Optimization intimidates some small business owners like me but after what I learned through your book I feel confident – for your own good get this book."

Julieta Alcantara, Mexican Masterpieces, LLC www.mexicanmasterpieces.net

GET TOP RANKING ON GOOGLE

& Other Search Engines

Grow Your Business – Online

By

Greg Bright

Small Business Owner / Consultant & Author of #1 Ranked Websites

**Your Customers Are Looking For You
Will You Be Found?**

Greg Bright – Publisher
Contact us via our website:
www.get-top-ranking-on-search-engines.com

First Edition – Published Fall 2008

ISBN 978-0-615-25199-8

Greg Bright is available for seminars and consulting engagements:

www.get-top-ranking-on-search-engines.com

To My Father.

Thanks Dad – For instilling my entrepreneurial spirit at such a young age. For driving my work ethic by expecting so much – for the countless life and business lessons.

Although the internet has changed and influenced business in many ways, the basics of business that you taught me still work.

(Dad passed away unexpectedly, right after receiving the manuscript for this book. As usual, I was counting on him for advice and editing help. At least he got to see this dedication to him. His spirit lives on through all that he touched – as he was a remarkable man – and the ultimate retailer.)

ACKNOWLEDGEMENTS

First to my beautiful wife for believing in my dream (and then actually letting me live it) and for standing by me through it all.

Many people helped with this book or influenced it in some way, from the friends that asked me to help them with their websites in past years to recent folks who gave support and editing advice.

To Sonia St. James for her encouragement over the years, introducing me to Lulu.com (publishing service), showing me the way, and editing.

To Hall Martin for all the years of advice and support – and inspiring me to think about my audience, and editing.

Thanks to these folks for their editing help: Jeffrey Lorien, Mary King, Jack Bright (in spirit), Sue Anne Bright (wife), Penny McConnell, James E. Dion, Martha Baker, and William Schroyer at www.RapidPressRelease.com.

Disclaimer and Other Legal Stuff

Contents

Chapter 3
KEYWORDS KEYWORDS KEYWORDS   41

Introduction

"I thought a lot about my intended audience for this book and came to the conclusion that it was small business owners with little or no internet marketing or web design experience." – Greg Bright

My wife and I run our businesses, by ourselves. Technically, our businesses are Micro Businesses, also known as a Mom and Pop businesses.

With our businesses located in Austin, Texas, I tend to get caught up in the technical jargon and buzzwords thrown around in some of the networking groups I belong to (Austin is a very "techie" city). I did not want to speak that same jargon to my audience, if they could not relate to it.

When I first circulated the rough draft of this book around to some of my networking contacts, the feedback I got was "Shouldn't business owners hire out the things they don't do well – like website design and search engine optimization?"

I realized then that my audience was ***not*** the recently "funded" venture that had a fresh infusion of cash to go out and hire a full time website designer. My audience was ***not*** the "techies" with their techno jargon, acronyms and buzzwords. My audience was Micro Business owners who have to do everything themselves – just like my wife and I.

I don't know about you, but in our businesses my wife and I share the responsibilities of Bookkeeper, Accountant, Salesperson, HR Director, Technician, Janitor and yes, Website Designer.

Small business owners (and charitable causes) need an easy to understand/easy to implement process for gaining an advantage over the corporate giants in the internet world. How did I come to realize this? When I first started this process for my own business twelve years ago, no such manual existed. Sure there were (and still are) books on the subject written by programmers, for programmers. These programmers had tremendous skills in programming but lacked the fundamentals of real world business practices, especially at the Micro Business level.

This book was intentionally written to help anyone at any level (or no level) of website design knowledge, whether you are just preparing to organize your start up business or your neighbor's kid launched your website five years ago.

I am not a programmer, nor do I understand the basic programming language for website design (HTML) all that well. I **am**, however, very successful at getting my websites high ranking.

Truth is, you really don't have to know the programming language of websites to know how to optimize your website for search engines and customers. That would be the same as saying that you have to know the programming code of Microsoft® Windows® just to turn on your computer, or the programming code of Microsoft® Word just to type a letter.

There are website design programs out there classified as WYSIWYG programs – "**W**hat **Y**ou **S**ee **I**s **W**hat **Y**ou **G**et". This just means that as you type text on the web page, or insert a picture, the program displays (on your monitor screen) how the actual web page will look to users on the internet. Adobe® Dreamweaver® is one of these WYSIWYG programs. Dreamweaver® is very user friendly and intuitive.

This really isn't rocket science here. Computers are just a tool to help you succeed. Utilize your tool in the most efficient way you can, without having to go through a huge learning curve.

I tried to keep the book brief, at the most basic understanding level, and to the point. I tried to put myself back into my own shoes, twelve years ago, when I set out learning how to build a website and I knew nothing – back then it was sink or swim for me.

Optimizing your website to get higher search engine ranking just takes a little research and a little patience. It goes the same for optimizing your website for great customer service. They both involve the basic marketing skills you are already doing in going about the every day promotion of your business.

I plan to place the feedback and up-to-date Search Engine Optimization information on the website for this book – ***www.get-top-ranking-on-search-engines.com***. I also plan to come out with a new edition of this book every year, since the world of SEO changes constantly. So, if you don't understand something in this book, probably other people are asking the same questions and I will try to answer them on the website and improve the next edition of the book.

Please see the Website for Consulting / Speaking Engagements

www.get-top-ranking-on-search-engines.com

Please visit my website for contact information – feedback is always welcome.

Define: HTML (Hypertext Markup Language) The programming language that most websites are written in.

Tip: Throughout this book **I will notate tips** which will be "called out" in these "text" boxes and will define terms when necessary by the notation ***Define: XYZ***.

By the way, I don't see very many of those recently funded ventures doing most of the techniques that I will share with you here – probably because they are not doing their "due diligence" (jargon / buzzword). It's easier for them to just hire one of the many amateurs out there who promise to get them "High Ranking".

So, I direct this book to you, the Micro Business Owners/Mom and Pops who are the front line of our free enterprise system – the risk takers – the seed planters – the backbone of our economy. The best news (for me) is that there are a heck of a lot of you out there in the world. After all, I would like to sell a few of these books ☺

Why Write a Book on SEO & Online Customer Service?

When friends and acquaintances found out how successful I have been with my own websites, they asked me to help them get better ranking on search engines for their businesses. These friends knew I had attended the "SEO School of Hard Knocks" for the past twelve years, scratching and crawling my way up. Finally, I am at the top with numerous websites (see the end of this book). What started as a few notes to some friends kept growing until I had enough information for a small book.

I wanted the novice to be able to get some quick knowledge which could be implemented immediately without a lot of effort nor a steep learning curve. This makes my book unique.

My book also differs from other books on SEO in that my advice comes from a customer service perspective. After all, the ultimate goal is to build lifelong customers for your business. I have spent the last 33 years in customer service and had the ultimate retailer as a mentor – my father. Dad was very well respected in the Ace Hardware community – nationwide. Dad always put the customer first!

I also saw an opportunity to share some "insider" secrets and lesser-known techniques, which (to my amazement) are not utilized on most websites – even the corporate giants.

Define: SEO – SEO stands for "Search Engine Optimization" and involves designing your website to be search-engine-friendly with the goal of high ranking – so your website can be found on the internet through search engines. (more about SEO in the next section)

I highly recommend that all business owners take charge of their website and the constant updating of it. You don't want to have to turn to a website designer every time you want to make a change. If you make changes and updates to your website on a regular basis (which you should do at least every week), then your website designer could end up costing a fortune! Furthermore, does a website designer really understand your business the way you do? Can they make recommendations based on looking at your business in its entirety? Does a website designer know your customers like you do?

If you do hire a website designer, find one that asks you lots of questions about your business. The website designer should rely on you for input for the design of the website – it should be a combined effort. Find one that will show you how to make subtle changes/updates yourself, and only rely on them for major updates.

Tip: Web designers and business owners can utilize this book as a tool for the entire web design project.

Business Owners: please make your notes throughout this book and offer them to your web designer. It will help them design your site, based on your knowledge of your business.

Web Designers: please ask your clients to read this book. Their knowledge will improve your design efforts. Also, if you are interested in having your design services referred on our website – please contact us.

www.get-top-ranking-on-search-engines.com

Tip: A word on website designers. There are many great website designers out there. Unfortunately, there are more amateurs than there are people that actually know what they are doing.

Website designers tend to be tech people, and rightfully so. Some tech folks have tunnel vision for their specific programming skills and don't have the ability to take a "holistic" view of your business.

Just be careful if you do hire someone. Make sure your website designer listens to you and understands your business. Your website design should be a collaboration between you and the designer, with them accepting much input from you.

You should **always** retain the rights to your website, which include the actual Design Program (get a copy), Registration and Hosting. Be sure you have all of the access codes, expiration dates and passwords to the registration, hosting, and design program, in case your website designer disappears – it happens! The tips in this book should point you in the right direction and steer you clear of the amateurs.

If any website designer offers to get you immediate high ranking – RUN! Even if they do get you immediate high ranking, they have employed deceptive tricks to do it and could get your website banned from all search engines.

You and your web designer must also consider the three main elements needed in order for a website to function. First you have to write a program that gives birth to the website (website design program). Second, you have to register a name for your website (www.yourname.com also known as the URL), and finally you have to have your website "hosted" on the hard drive of a server on the internet – more on this later.

You can start with any tip or topic in this book. Just pick one that makes sense to you, take some baby steps and then master the next tip. There is no order to it. Don't worry if I mention a tip or talk about something that you don't understand. Just keep going. You will pick up many ideas throughout. Don't get "hung up" on any one particular topic.

Even if you don't want to take charge of your website yourself, this book will help you talk intelligently to your website designer. It will help you separate the players from the amateurs.

No one knows your business like you do, and it's up to you to keep it fresh. A fresh and consistently-updated website not only gets you higher ranking, your customers appreciate it as well, hopefully coming back for more.

Tip: Search engines penalize websites that have not been updated, since their last "spider" crawl. Therefore, plan to add something new every week – updated content, press release, newsletter, article or image file named with a keyword.

Define: Spider – Search engines have programs (called Spiders or "Bots") that go out and look at every single website on the internet. They "crawl" every aspect (including file names, text and the actual programming code), of every page of every website on the internet attempting to rank them by subject matter. They rank both the home page and the individual pages – mostly relating them to keywords that searchers might enter into the search box of the search engine. Again, the page being ranked could be the "Home Page" (the home page is the most important) or any other page within the website.

Internet Opportunity for Small Businesses

Etailing (online retail) was up another twenty plus percent as 2007 came to an end. Shoppers would much rather surf the internet than spend time in traffic and pay high gasoline prices driving all over the place. Even my wife bought all of our Christmas presents last year "online". Now, that might not mean a lot to you, but to me it's huge. It says a ton about the shopping habits of folks. We're talking about a woman that loves the retail shopping experience and did not order any gifts online the previous Christmas! Don't get me wrong, she still shops "brick and mortar" stores, but now she's pre-shopping the items (online) before she hits the road.

Define: Brick and Mortar Business – a brick and mortar business is a business in the traditional sense. It has a physical location, versus an internet business, which might only exist on the web.

Another opportunity for small business is that the internet is the perfect advertising / marketing vehicle. If you think about it, most advertising is intrusive. You're reading a news article and you have to navigate through all of the ads. You're watching TV and the commercials interrupt your experience. In contrast, internet shoppers are actually looking for your information. They are searching for your products!

I also feel that there is a paradigm shift going on out there in the "brick and mortar" retail store arena which will highlight the need for small business owners to have a better web presence. Back when my family and I owned our Ace Hardware stores (and also when I moved on to work for Ace Corporate in the early 90's as a retail consultant), the experts said that there was simply too much retail square footage in the United States, for the population to support it.

Well, retailers just kept on building! There are some pretty large egos at work. (For example, you might have seen major home centers built right across the street from one another.) The bottom line is that there is going to be some fallout – which small business owners can take advantage of, if they are prepared, and if they can be found on the internet.

Compounding the "overbuilding" fact is that the "Big Box" stores have to draw from a very large market area, requiring some of their customers to drive quite a distance to get to them. With high gas prices, customers are going to start cocooning around their neighborhoods more and more, benefiting independently owned – local Mom and Pop businesses. To be sure, customers are becoming thriftier in their shopping escapades and doing much of the "leg work" of the shopping on the internet prior to hitting the road.

It's not enough for Mom and Pop businesses to simply have a website on the internet. They have to be found through the search engines allowing the customer to "pre-shop" their store inventories, in preparation for stopping by the physical location for a purchase.

Internet retailing is much more than just making a sale on your website "online". It's about acquiring and building customer relationships that can turn into lifelong purchases at your "brick and mortar" location.

Furthermore, society is becoming "surrounded" by the internet. The "Low Cost" laptop market segment is gaining some unexpected steam. (I try to stay on top of the laptop market for my patented Laptop Stand invention at Keynamics® LLC www.keynamics.com.) This low cost laptop segment is good news for both you and I. Laptop manufacturers are talking about coming out with a laptop that costs under $100 in the near future. Talk about putting the internet everywhere! Market researchers are estimating that 145 million laptops will be sold in 2008. That's up from 100 million units in 2007 and 80 million in 2006. Everyone will have a laptop eventually. Even people who already own one will be getting a second and third just to throw around, say in the trunk of the car, a gym bag, under the car seat. You can even get a pretty good version of the internet on cell phones these days. The point is that the internet is truly everywhere, meaning customers everywhere can have access to your business 24/7. Will you be found?

Whether you sell a product on the internet (etailing), offer a service, or run a charitable/worthwhile cause, it's all the same. To be successful, it's not a matter of *if* you will have a strong internet presence, *it's when*. That when is now.

Before moving on to the main part of the book, I would like to mention a few programs that I personally use. I only point them out so that you know my perspective and my point of view from the various examples given. I use the Microsoft® Windows® (operating system), Microsoft® Internet Explorer® (web browser), Adobe Photoshop® (photo editing program), Adobe Dreamweaver ® (website design program) and Google™ (search engine).

> **Tip:** Maybe your sales mainly come from your "brick and mortar" storefront. Even if you don't actually sell much on the internet, many of your customers are researching products on the internet first, then going to a "brick and mortar" store to make the purchase. Plus, another revenue stream (from online sales) sure couldn't hurt ☺

Define: Micro Business — Technically, a small business as defined by the SBA has less than $5 million in sales and less than 500 employees. A Micro Business might have zero employees and can be run by one or two people (typically family members). I tend to view a Micro Business and a "Mom and Pop" business as one in the same.

> **Tip:** You can find the definition of anything on the internet using Google, by typing **(define: "XYZ")**. Put in the colon, but omit the parenthesis and quotation marks and insert the word or words where the "XYZ" is. So, if I do use a word or term in this book that you don't understand, go to Google and get it defined.

Part I:
Optimizing
For GOOGLE
&
Other
Search Engines

"Optimizing for Google also optimizes for the rest of the search engines" – Greg Bright

Chapter 1

What is SEO and How Can it Help Your Business?

If you are one of those people (like me) that skip the introduction of most books, please go back and read it – instructions are given there that will guide you through the rest of this book.

Micro Businesses or Mom and Pop businesses are perfect for marketing and selling on the internet for numerous reasons. For example, you can cater to a niche, something that is difficult for larger corporations which are most interested in turning fast moving items to the masses. You can focus on a few of your most important "niche" items. Larger chains can't focus because they have such a huge inventory which changes constantly. Larger enterprises also have to be broader in scope which dilutes their efforts on the web.

A Micro Business isn't tied down to bureaucratic red tape. It can implement new ideas and changes quickly without having to get approval from upper management, go through several committees, then get stuck in the Legal department or (worse yet) the Finance department.

Micro Businesses engage with and listen to the customer, something that upper management of larger corporations has a hard time with because of all of the layers. This "front line" knowledge provides better insight, understanding, and responsiveness.

Business basics don't change with technology. Small business owners know how to cater to and "Love their Customers to Death" (Dad-ism). Mom and Pops can rely on their wisdom of good businesses practices and customer service much better than the latest "Virtual Store". After all, who is the local shopper going to trust? The local community folks they drive by every day, or the mega-store in cyberspace? Parlay this business wisdom into your website design, both when optimizing for search engines and optimizing for customers.

Furthermore, web surfers pay a lot more attention to the "Natural Listings" because they know these listings are relevant to their searches and not simply "paid for" advertising. This is the same principle as "Ad Blindness" where readers of print materials simply "tune out" all of the ads.

Another advantage is that most search engines run on a philosophy of democracy. Meaning, the huge corporations can't "out spend" you, or influence the search outcome of the "Natural Search" results.

Define: Natural Search Results – Most search engines return about ten individual website results on the first page after a searcher types a keyword into the search box – this is called the Search Engine Results Page – SERP. The individual ten listings are referred to as the "natural" search results. Do not confuse them with the sponsored (paid advertising) links that are usually listed on the right side of the page with a few sometimes listed just above the natural results. These "advertisements" are usually indicated as "Paid" or "Sponsored" ads. Natural search results are free.

All of these advantages level the playing field on the internet for Micro Businesses. In reality, you have the upper hand against the corporate giants! With a little time and effort you can outrank the large corporations on search engines – especially in your niche areas.

What is SEO?

We are talking about Search Engine Optimization also known as SEO or "Website Optimization". Basically, this involves designing and programming your website to be search-engine-friendly with the goal of high "natural" ranking on the first page of the search results (search engine results page – SERP).

Of course, we have to balance the need for search engine rank with a little common sense. We do still want to attract the paying customers to our site. Therefore, apply basic internet marketing principles as well (explained in Part II).

There is an entire industry created by professionals who do this, and charge for it. There are varied opinions out there as to what works and what does not work, and there are some hard and fast rules which can be followed. But remember, the information is proprietary and changes daily. To help keep yourself constantly updated, subscribe to various newsletters and magazines on the topic of SEO and perform routine Google searches on SEO.

Google is very secretive about what algorithms they use to index websites. Algorithms are plugged into the computer programs that rank websites, but I am certain that Google has a lot more "Human" involvement in website ranking than they would admit. Why? Because they can afford to hire the people to manually look at a lot of websites and rank them based on relevancy. Just one more reason to employ only legitimate techniques for high ranking.

Define: Algorithms – The rules that search engines use to rank webpages.

Tip: Before I make *any* change or add *anything* new to my website, first and foremost, I think about how it will affect my ranking. I evaluate every single step and keystroke for SEO. ** It's also imperative that you save the previous version of your website, before you make any changes. Save it to an external media (like a CD) to be held in safe keeping off site.

Relevance

Try to put yourself in Google's shoes. What is Google's main philosophy, and why do most of us love using the Google search engine so much? Because the search engine provides a good experience by returning results that are ***relevant*** to our search words.

An Example of Non-Relevance:

I sell my patented laptop stand and I know that Hewlett-Packard (HP) sells a lot of laptops. Therefore, I would love for everyone who searches for an HP laptop to land on my webpage and learn how my laptop stand can help them use their laptops more comfortably. So, I could optimize my website with the keywords "HP Laptop", in hopes that everyone searching for this would end up on my site. Wishful thinking – but "laptop stands" are not very relevant to a search for "HP Laptops" and Google would never rank me very high for those keywords.

Google even ranks its paid search results or "sponsored links" (It's called the Google AdWords™ Program) by relevance to the searcher's search words. In short, you can't "buy" your way to the top of the sponsored links list. Pretty cool, huh? Again, it levels the playing field.

One way Google measures the relevance (on the Natural Search Results and the AdWords program) is by how often a searcher clicks on any particular website (or sponsored link) in relation to other sponsored links or websites. They assume that more people clicking on your website must mean it is more relevant to that particular search keyword (or phrase) that the searcher typed into the Google search box.

Bottom Line: There are some commonly known things that will help you with Google (and all the rest of the search engines). There are also many deceptive things which can get you banned from Google altogether (or penalized, so you show up on page 100).

The idea is to show up on page one, two, or three on the "natural" (and free) search results. Page one or two being the best on most search engines. As of 2008, Google commands more than 60% of the search engine market, with Yahoo!® next, then MSN® Internet Services. Anything after page three on any search engine is pretty much worthless.

Tip: What you do to "Optimize" your site on Google, helps you on all the rest of the search engines too.

I will share some techniques that I have learned over the years, but I also strongly suggest that you start your own research project. You will gather the best information from the internet itself by searching for "SEO". This should be a never ending research project because the search engines are constantly changing.

What to Expect

Everyone reading this book probably has a different expectation of the success level that they can achieve in their businesses or organizations using the internet. It might help if I give you a range of expectations to shoot for. Aim high!

If you are selling a very popular or competitively branded item like the iPod®, for example, do not expect to be ranked number one for that keyword any time in this century. It just won't happen. I'd love for you to prove me wrong on this, but let's be realistic. However, you *might* expect high ranking for some unique niche service you offer based on the iPod®.

You should expect to be ranked number one for the basic things like a search for your business name, or a search for your business service or product along with the keywords of your town or area. Building upon that, the sky is the limit!

You should also expect that once visitors get to your website, you will convert them into paying customers, get them to call on the phone, or convince them to walk into your physical location. You can do all this by utilizing good internet retailing practices.

High ranking will not happen overnight, probably not even within the first year. In fact, some people refer to the Google "Sandbox". They say that Google and other search engines purposely keep new websites at a lower ranking for the first several months after launching a new website. This does make sense, if you think about it. Google wants to supply their users with the most relevant search results. Most times, new businesses are still trying to work out the "kinks" during the first year of operations, plus this keeps "fly-by-night" businesses from competing with legitimate businesses. Search engines figure that a more "seasoned" business will have the experience to serve the customer better. ***So start early!***

Tip: Free Business Listing with Google

This simple tip might be the quickest easiest thing you can do to get your business at the top. It mainly works for targeting local customers, if that's your target market.

Use the Google **"Local Business Center"** to create your free listing. When potential customers do a regular web search or use "Google Maps" for local information, they'll find your business, your address, hours of operation, even photos of your storefront or products. This is part of "Google Maps" but it works on a regular Google "web" search too.

(Note – "Google Maps" is one of the advanced Google search areas found at the top left of the main Google search page. These are great tools to refine your searches on Google. Want to find an obscure or out of print book? Try "Google Books" under the "more" arrow.)

To start the business listing process, you have to create a Google account (which is free). You must be able to receive regular postal mail at your business address. Google will physically mail a pin code to your address, verifying that you are really there. Once you get the pin, you respond and they add you. It's like a yellow page business listing on Google. They list you by the business category and town you are in.

Google is building its own business listings from local yellow page listings and other sources. But *why wait* for them and why depend on them (or your local yellow pages company) to get your business category right? Be proactive and submit it yourself. You can also include lots of other pertinent information about your business – like coupons and web links to your website.

Find out about Google's business listing service @

http://www.google.com/local/add/

Yahoo® offers something similar:

http://listings.local.yahoo.com/csubmit/index.php

Chapter Action Steps / Notes

1. What to Expect (set your goals here).

_____

_____

_____

_____

2. Think about what separates your business from the competition (be thinking about keywords and text that are relevant to your uniqueness).

_____

_____

_____

_____

3. Apply for Local Business Listing on Google.

_____

_____

_____

_____

Chapter 2

How to Get Banned From Search Engines

(Or Severely Penalized)

Invisible Text and Other Deceptive Tricks

Since text is very important to the search engine spiders, some people add a bunch of repetitive keywords or other commonly searched for text and make it the same color as the background (this text is usually irrelevant to their website). Therefore, the spiders see it, but human eyes don't. From my previous example: I could repeat "HP Laptop" a thousand times in the same color text as my background and never have it be seen by human eyes. The spiders would see it and think "This site must sell a bunch of HP Laptops, so let's give them high ranking on the search term of HP Laptop." Some cheaters make the text so small that human eyes can't read it, but the spiders still can. Some cheaters try "keyword stuffing" – placing too many keywords in your text and other places.

Link Sharing (maybe not banned but banished to page 100)

Never ***ever*** agree to share links or join a link sharing group or farm – you will get penalized. Link sharing groups trade links with each other, with the sole purpose of tricking the search engines into thinking that a website has a bunch of incoming links. "Hey, I will link to your website, if you link to mine". While the quantity of incoming links might be there, they are ***not*** relevant incoming links. All of the search engines have figured out this one so don't do it. ***Do*** encourage others in your industry to link to your site. These are called incoming links (or backlinks) and Google places a very high value on ***RELEVANT*** incoming links from other reputable websites in your industry (more on this later).

Define: Incoming Links – Incoming links are when any other website has created a clickable hyperlink to your website.

These are also referred to as "Backlinks". Hyperlink and Link are used interchangeably.

Duplicate Sites (Severely Penalized)

This seems to be a little known fact. Google penalizes you if you have "Duplicate Sites". Duplicate sites are two or more different website addresses (URLs) that have the exact same content (graphics and text). I learned this the hard way by trying to have ***www.laptop-ergonomics.com*** and ***www.keynamics.com*** be the same exact websites for the first 18 months after launching. Everything was uploaded verbatim to each separate site, resulting in duplicate sites. Researching SEO one day, I ran across numerous articles on this duplicate site thing. It was only when I started varying both the content and image file names on both sites that they both finally started creeping up in ranking. I have had high ranking for the search of "laptop ergonomics" for three years running now that I fixed the duplication error.

Also, do not have two separate pages in your website with the same content, as this could be considered a duplicate site and penalized.

Define: URL — URL stands for Uniform Resource Locator and is the part of the web address between the www. and the .com

It's the address that people find you by when pulling up your website on the internet, also known as the domain name.

Tip: About a year ago, I changed hosting companies to a prominent hosting company. I did not realize it, but one of my obscure URLs (I have a bunch registered) somehow got tied in with my main website, therefore creating a duplicate site totally unknown to me. Boy, I immediately saw lower ranking until I fixed it!

I knew this had something to do with switching hosting companies, because my ranking started to fall immediately after the hosting switch. According to the experts, the mere act of switching a hosting company should not affect your ranking. It's also interesting to note that during my conversations with the representatives about the logistics of switching, one of them actually recommended that I create a temporary duplicate site so I would not have any downtime during the switch over. So, even the so called "experts" can lead you down the wrong path!

Define: Hosting Company – A hosting company actually "hosts" (or stores) your website program files (usually along with other website customers' program files) on a hard drive on their server. Servers allow your website to be accessed by internet users on the world wide web. They usually charge a "rental" fee for this service based on your website size and traffic. This negates the need to have your own server, which would have to be professionally maintained. Some things are wise to rent out.

Keyword Stuffing

Define: Keyword Stuffing – Repeating keywords over and over in certain areas of your website – stuffing it full of keywords. This usually penalizes you. For example, you will get penalized if you repeat a bunch of keywords in your keyword meta tag or in the body of your text on any webpage (more on Meta tags later).

Google employs something called LSI (Latent Semantic Indexing). In simple terms, it just means that they don't look at the number of times a keyword is repeated on a page. They look at how the keyword is associated with the "theme" or context of the page. Therefore, write good quality text that makes sense to your audience. Squeeze in as many darn keywords as you can, ***while*** keeping it logical and grammatically correct☺.

Don't use Special Characters or Punctuation

In important fields like files names or meta tags, special characters can cause trouble (more on this and meta tags later). Special characters are any non-alphabetical or non-numerical characters including (but not limited to) - spaces, periods, comas, and quotation marks. Search Engine spiders have a hard time with special characters and spaces in your web address. Many search engines will not even index your site if it contains special characters in the "text" links.

> **Tip:** Make sure all of the links to your other web pages (from your homepage and amongst themselves) are text links, not an image or graphic link. Otherwise, you will NOT get indexed!

Define: Text Link — A link (or hyperlink) is simply a way to jump from one webpage to another, whether it's within the various pages of your site or linking outside to another website. A link is typically designated by the arrow on your pointer changing to a hand once placed over the link. The link can be a picture (or image) or it can be actual text. If it's text it can be composed of keywords, or it can be the actual web address of the page it's going to. Using "text" links, composed of your important keywords is the *only* way to go (more on this later). You can always tell if it's a text link by being able to highlight the actual text (for example if you wanted to copy and paste the text). You can't highlight text from a picture link — because there is not any text there. Also, text links are usually underlined and usually change color when your mouse pointer runs over them.

Tip: Text might not actually be real text. What?? OK, imagine taking a picture of a roadside billboard and placing that picture on your website. Yeah, the billboard has some text on it, but it's still a picture. Humans can read that text, but search engine spiders have no way of reading it if it's an actual picture. Therefore, many images can have text in them, but it's really not text. Take care that you do not give up valuable keywords by having an image of text instead of actual text. It's better to replace the image with actual text, or to place the text over the image in your website design program, so it's real text. Clear as mud, huh?

Company logos are actually pictures, so if your company name is on your logo, don't expect the spiders to pick up these very important keywords (your actual company name).

This is also why it's important to name the picture file with a keyword (more in the next chapter).

Define: Index —Indexing is just a fancy word meaning that a particular search engine has included your website within its search results. In other words, they have found you.

You Must Have a "Contact Us" TEXT Link from Your Home Page

Many search engines will not index a website if it does not have a "contact" page linking from the home page (and it does have to be a text link). Your contact page should list your phone number, email address, and a physical address (physical addresses are better than PO boxes – it builds the trust factor among visitors).

Don't use a "Splash" Page

Most search engines penalize for a splash page. Customers don't like them either. Your home page of your website should be the actual home page, sometimes called the "Index" page and should be the first page a visitor lands on upon visiting your website. An exception to this is if you want to optimize specific keywords for a specific page within your website (more on this in chapter three).

Tip: Your home page should be listed as the "index" page in your web design program and on your hosting server.

Define: Splash Page – These are pages that usually have some sort of fancy video, music or Adobe® Flash® Player animation that visitors must sit through first, before they can "Click to Enter" the main "Real" website.

Define: Hosting Server –The internet is just a bunch of servers connected to each other worldwide. These servers are nothing more than a fancy version of your home personal computer. They are typically stacked on top of one another and the company that ***hosts*** websites might have rows and rows of these "stacks". Your website program will be "hosted" on one of those servers. Most of us rent that space on a "shared" server, meaning that we share the hard drive space (on one of the servers) with many other websites that are hosted on that same server's hard drive.

No Broken Links

If your site contains ***ANY*** broken links, you could risk not being listed (or indexed) by the search engines.

Define: Broken Link – A link that does not work. You click on it and you get a blank webpage that says something like "Internet Explorer cannot display the webpage".

Bottom Line on Upsetting the Google Search Gods

Google has figured out all the tricks. If you (or your website designer) try to do something deceptive they ***will*** eventually catch you.

Don't worry! There are numerous perfectly legitimate techniques that you can use to get higher ranking, more traffic, and improved customer service – all at the same time.

Tip: You can register your URL with the major search engines. I believe that this is a moot point, because the natural process will find a properly optimized site – mainly through high quality (and relevant) incoming links from other websites within your industry. Those Google spiders follow links from other sites to yours and then you are indexed! This process does not take long, so start *fishing* for backlinks early (chapter 4).

To find out if you have been found (indexed) by Google, just type your full web address (*www.keynamics.com*) in the Google search box. If they know about you, you will show up in the search results. *Beware:* Do not pay someone to add your site for you. Do it yourself for free.

On Google:

http://www.google.com/addurl/

On Yahoo®:
http://search.yahoo.com/info/submit.html

On MSN:

http://search.msn.com.sg/docs/submit.aspx

Tip: SEO experts have said that it is hard for any search engine to crawl and properly index Adobe Flash files. Google and Adobe recently announced a new algorithm to fix the problem. You can read about it here:

http://googleblog.blogspot.com/2008/06/google-learns-to-crawl-flash.html

This "fix" was announced in June of 2008. According to some SEO experts, they have not worked all the "bugs" out.

I personally use a Flash file on my *www.keynamics.com* site (it's the photo slideshow on the very top of the home page). Flash is a wonderful tool and can enhance the visitor's experience by adding animation, video and interactivity to web pages.

However, I would proceed with caution when it comes to using too much Flash. A little is OK, but stay away from websites designed 100% with Flash.

Chapter Action Steps / Notes

1. You should not have any of these: (invisible text – links from link sharing farms – duplicate sites – overuse of keywords – picture links instead of text links – broken links – splash page)

_____

_____

_____

_____

2. Do you have a "Contact Us" link on your home page? Is it a text link?

_____

_____

_____

_____

3. Has your website been indexed? Do you want to submit/register it with the major search engines?

_____

_____

_____

_____

Chapter 3

KEYWORDS
KEYWORDS
KEYWORDS

A wise old Search Engine Optimization specialist once told me: "The three most important things in Search Engine Optimization are: Keywords, Keywords, and Keywords"

Define: Keyword —A keyword is any word (or phrase) that a searcher might type into the search box of any search engine.

The Most Important Thing Regarding Keywords

Is to decide what main keyword or keyword "phrase" you want for your home page so you are sure to get high ranking for that keyword.

My sister is a dental hygienist and her dentist wanted some SEO advice. The dentist wanted to be sure to show up for any search keywords comprised of "Dentist (and their town name)". I took a quick look at her website and noticed that they only mentioned the town name in a couple of places (and some of those were images with no actual text). I suggested they put the town name everywhere (without overdoing it) in all image file names, meta tags, alt tags, URL addresses, and work it into the body text (visible text) of each individual webpage – especially the first couple of sentences. They implemented most of my suggestions and slowly started moving up in ranking for the search of "Dentist (and their town name)".

On my own laptop stand website, I wanted to show up number one for the search of "Laptop Stand". You should decide what keywords are most important for every page "within" your website – not just your homepage.

For Example, on a page of my Keynamics® website, I sell BodyBilt office chairs. On that page "BodyBilt office chairs" is the most important keyword "phrase". (By the way, keywords can also mean "keyword phrases" which are several words strung together that a searcher might be typing in the Google search box.) I also sell Plantronics® headsets and, you guessed it, on that page "Plantronics headsets" is most important.

Coming up with keywords can be a challenge and will take the most time and effort of a good website optimization program. Don't just rely on your own insight. As Dad often said, "Sometimes we can't see the forest through the trees".

In order to get a good sampling of all web searchers, ask your customers and friends how they would search for items you sell. Even ask people with little or no experience in web search – not just the folks with online experience.

Try to figure out what words the lay person is using, not just the latest jargon from your industry. For example, the technically correct term for a portable computer is "notebook computer". However, they are most commonly referred to as "laptops". I decided early on that it was more important to feature "Laptop Stand" than the more politically correct term "Notebook Stand" for my invention.

Another good source of keyword popularity is the internet itself. Try the tools at the major search engines as well as sites like: ***https://adwords.google.com/select/KeywordToolExternal***

www.dmoz.org   ***www.overture.com***
www.wordtracker.com and ***www.nichebot.com*** .

Naming Files

Websites and all of their individual components are simply a bunch of strung-together files – and files have to be named, but not with just any old name. Name them with a keyword!

Every single file in your website should have a keyword in it!

Make it easy for the spider programs to find your keywords on your website. File names hold a high priority with search engine spiders. Little things like naming all of your files something significant (ideally a keyword or "keyword phrase" that someone might search for) really add up.

An example of a file name with keywords:

http://www.keynamics.com/laptop_stand_press.htm

This is the file name (which also happens to be the URL) for my "press" page which includes high resolution pictures for the press to download, press releases and other newsworthy items that I think an editor might be interested in when doing a story on us. (I simply direct any press inquiries to this page, making it easier for them to do a story on my business. Making an editor's job easier increases the likelihood that they will write your story.) Most web designers would have simply named this page *http://www.keynamics.com/press.htm.*. Notice how I squeezed in more keywords the way I did it.

Tip: Having a Google AdWords™ program (paid sponsor links) is a great way to find out what keywords people are searching for within your industry on the internet. I have spent over $10,000 with the Google Adwords program over the years and, while I get a return on my investment from an advertising standpoint, the best return I get is finding out which keywords people are currently searching. I probably have over 1,000 keywords in my AdWords program. You don't have to spend a lot of money to start a Google Adwords™ campaign, and you will gather tons of marketing research! You can run a keyword report any way you want to on your Google AdWords™ program. Very, very useful tool!

The really cool thing is that once you start getting high natural search ranking for a particular keyword, you can stop paying for sponsored links for that keyword. For example, I spent thousands of dollars in the beginning for the keyword "Laptop Stand". Now that I rank high for the search of "Laptop Stand", I don't advertise it at all on AdWords. What would be the point? "Laptop Stand" happens to be a very competitive keyword. Google Adwords™ charges by the competitiveness of the keyword. They charge each time a searcher clicks on your ad and goes to your website. This is what they mean by "Pay Per Click". I average about 50 cents per bid (and it is a bidding thing) on all of my Google keywords. Hmm – A Google AdWords™ book could be next ☺

Achieving high ranking on the natural search results is like free advertising.

Image File Names

Every picture file (also called an image file) in your website should have a significant name related to your keyword strategy.

To name a file is the same as giving it a name when you save the file to a folder. A typical saved image file name on a website would look like ***laptop_stand.jpg***, which is usually stored in the images file folder of your website design program. (Or maybe you have it in your "My Pictures" folder stored under your "My Documents" folder, waiting to be moved to your image file folder on your website design program.) When it appears in your website it is also stored (usually) in your "Images" file folder on the server which hosts your website. So, ultimately it might look something like:

http://www.keynamics.com/images/laptop_stand.jpg
Think of each forward slash as a division up to the next file folder level of storage.

The following analogy of how you would file a piece of paper might help with the file structure of a website:

The ***http://*** is the entire world, the ***www.keynamics.com*** is your office address. Your website design "program files" are all stored in the filing cabinet in your office and the actual picture file ***laptop_stand.jpg*** is a file within your images folder in your file cabinet. Whereas the ***http://*** relates to the World Wide Web, the

www.keynamics.com is your registered URL address (possibly, but not necessarily, registered with the same company that hosts your website). The web design program files are stored on the hard drive of a server hosted by your hosting company. The actual image is stored in the "images" file (within your website program) on your hosted server. It's all just a hierarchy of files strung together forming the website and ultimately the World Wide Web.

Tip: I can't believe how many prominent websites miss out on naming their image files with significant keywords.

If you don't think naming picture files is important, then why does Google (and all the others) have an entire search engine devoted to ranking images? Look at the top left on the Google search home page. See the "images" link? I have countless pictures from my websites on the first page of results there, and I know it's just from naming the picture files with a relevant keyword.

Most web designers are too busy to do this, as it does take more thought and time than just naming your image "homepage image 1".

Naming files can be a little trickier than it would seem. For example, I have a lot of image files on my website with (laptop_stand) in the file name. You have to get creative to keep them all different, while also organized by name for your own clarity. It does not matter what's after the keyword in the file name as long as you place an underscore (or hyphen) after the last letter of the keyword. (But make sure the keywords come first) One file name could be **laptop_stand_black.jpg** and another **laptop_stand_123.jpg**. There is a limit as to how many characters you can have in a file name and your website design program will truncate after you have reached the limit, so play around with the keywords used in file names.

Tip: Right click on any of your competitors' images, then click on "properties" to display their file name. It's a quick test to find out if they know this technique – and you can find out their keyword strategy as well.

You can name many things in your website that are not actually pictures but still have file names. For example, borders, artwork, and various shapes that comprise the theme of your website. You can easily name all of these elements with an important keyword file name. Make sure to separate the words (if you have more than one word in your file name) with either underscores or hyphens, but never just string the words together and never use spaces to separate the words in a file name.

> **Tip:** There is some debate out there as to which one works the best (hyphens or underscores) in file names, so I use both equally.

> **Tip:** There is also some debate about whether the characters in the file name should contain any capital letters. To be safe, I just stick to all lower case in my file naming scheme.

An example on naming files:

Right:

http://www.keynamics.com/ergonomic_office_chairs_body bilt.htm

Wrong:

http://www.keynamics.com/ergonomicofficechairsbodybilt .htm

http://www.keynamics.com/ergonomic_office_c hairs_bodybilt.htm is the file name of my BodyBilt chair page. This always appears in the address bar in your browser (Microsoft® Internet Explorer®, etc.). It is very important to separate the keywords in the file name within the actual URL by hyphens before the ".com" and underscores after the forward slash "/". Internet Protocol (the rules) only allows hyphens to be used to separate words in the main URL of a web address (this is the part between the www and the .com). No spaces or underscores are allowed in this area of the web address.

The search engine spiders can read keywords more easily if you separate the words with hyphens versus all the words running together.

Text Links

It is important to use text, with your actual keywords in it, as the actual link to various pages within your website, instead of an image link. For example, most of my links to various pages of my website from my home page run across the top of the page. The link to the BodyBilt chair page is a text link (not a graphic or picture). The text is simply "BodyBilt Office Chairs".

> **Tip:** A hyperlink can be attached to an image or the actual text on a webpage.

Define: Hyperlink – A hyperlink is any link that opens another page on the internet from your current page, typically designated by the little arrow on your pointer changing to a hand.

Meta Tags and Keywords

All websites have "Meta Tags" in the source (programming) code.

Define: Meta Tags – programming code that works in the background of any website, the most common being HTML – Hypertext Markup Language.

There are three important meta tags: The ***Title*** meta tag, the ***Keyword*** meta tag and the ***Description*** meta tag.

Example of how a keyword meta tag looks in your programming code:

```
<meta name="keywords" content="laptop stand, airline in-flight internet, portable, travel, notebook, ergonomic, workstation, holder, platform, tray, accessories, riser, wrist pain, keyboard, neutral postures, carpal tunnel syndrome, repetitive stress injuries, neck pain, laptop heat, posture">
```

You should have the option to fill out "Title Meta Tags", "Keyword Meta tags" & "Description Meta tags" in your website design program. Your website design program (or programmer) can set these up for you.

The ***Title*** meta tag appears on the very top bar of the browser (Internet Explorer®) window when you view a webpage.

> **Tip:** To see what keywords your competitors are using in their meta tags, click "View" at the top of Microsoft® Internet Explorer® and then click "Source". This reveals the source code (HTML code) of any webpage.
>
> It's a great idea to do this to your competitors or others in your industry who have high ranking (why reinvent the wheel?). It's a good way to find out what keywords and other techniques are working for them.

Don't overdo keywords in meta tags or you will get penalized. Only put about 30 keywords in your keyword meta tag and do not repeat a keyword. Separate keywords by commas.

The **Description** meta tag should be a couple of sentences and again, do not repeat keywords or you will get penalized.

> **Tip:** Experts say these keyword and description meta tags are not as important as they used to be because everyone stuffs a bunch of keywords in them, but you should still have them – especially the description meta tag (more on this later).

ALT Tags

Define: Alt Tags – Alt tags are the little boxes of text that show up when you hold your cursor over any picture on a website. ALT stands for "alternative text" and helps the visually impaired.

Alt tags are mainly for the handicapped, but all search engines place a major importance on this. They reward your site for being handicap friendly. The ALT tags should use five or six significant keywords; do not stuff it with repetitive keywords. Again, your website design program should allow you to create an ALT tag for every image. (It's OK for ALT tags to have spaces between the words, but don't use special characters.)

Naming Your "Other" (Not the Home page) Web Pages

Every individual webpage on your site is actually a file. It should be named something important and have its own individual Title, Keyword and Description Meta Tags. (Many websites just copy the meta tags from the home page to all of the other pages – what a missed opportunity.)

For example, my page that describes the BodyBilt line of chairs is named:

http://www.keynamics.com/ergonomic_office_chairs _bodybilt.htm .

This is worth repeating from earlier. Notice that the file name to link this page (from our home page) after the ".com/" is actual keywords separated by underscores. Every webpage linked from your home page (which is also called the index page) should be set up like this, with underscores between the keywords.

If it's not too late, Start Out With A Main URL That Contains Keywords

If you can, name your doman ***www.your-name.com*** with keywords separated by hyphens (and they have to be hyphens). For example, I just started another business manufacturing concrete countertops and concrete furniture. I named my business "Ancient Art Concrete Countertops". I could have named it Greg's Countertops, but that would not have been as effective in capitalizing on my most important keywords – "Concrete Countertops".

Furthermore, instead of having my domain named ***www.ancientartconcretecountertops.com,*** I named it ***www.ancient-art-concrete-countertops.com***. Notice the dashes (hyphens) between the words. The dashes make it easier for search engine spiders to find, plus it's easier for people to read.

*Note: I also registered ***www.ancientartconcretecountertops.com*** so no one else could take it.

If you have already established some history with your current web address, do not change it. Remember that new web addresses are subject to the Google sandbox for a few months.

Tip: If you really want to go keyword crazy, start out by naming your company with keywords in it. For example, I just formed a new entity to handle my Aviator Laptop Stand. I needed it to be a separate company from my main business (Keynamics® LLC). I incorporated it with the name "Laptop Stands Inc." This will not only help with the website for this new company, it will help potential and current vendors find us easier within their internal systems. After all, they are just saving me as a vendor, in a file, somewhere in their system, so the file might as well be – you guessed it, a keyword.

Some people ask, "but doesn't it take too long to type in your website address with all of those hyphens between the words?" Fact is, most people who find your website find it by linking to it from another website or search engine, so it does not matter – they never actually have to type in your web address. I am also fortunate enough to be able to tell my customers how to get to my website by just searching "Concrete Countertops Austin" on Google. We are number one right now.

Launch Additional Websites with Your Keywords in the URL

You can create entirely new websites with your keywords in the URL, then link them back to your main URL. Just be careful not to duplicate any content – verbatim.

For example, I have the following additional, completely separate websites all linked back to my main website of ***www.keynamics.com*** :

www.laptop-ergonomics.com

www.keyboard-ergonomics.com

www.office-chair-ergonomics.com

Tip: When registering your domain name, register it for more than just one year. Your registrar will give you the option of paying for one year or multiple years. Search Engines reward websites that they know are going to be around for a while.

Chapter Action Steps / Notes

1. What Keyword (or keyword phrase) is the most important to your unique business qualities/services/products? More importantly – what keywords are your customers using to search for your unique qualities/services/products? These keywords should be emphasized everywhere on your home page – without overusing them. Go through this exercise for each individual webpage within your website.

_____

_____

_____

_____

2. Right click on your image files. What are they named? If they are composed of several keywords, are they separated by hyphens or underscores?

_____

_____

_____

_____

3. Are your links to all of the pages within your website "text" links – with your most important keywords in them?

_____

_____

4. Right click on your competitors images. Also, look at their meta tags (view – source in Internet Explorer) for good keyword ideas.

_____

_____

_____

_____

5. Does your Title meta tag have an attention grabbing "headline" with good use of your keywords? Does your Description meta tag compel users to go to your website with a "call to action" while also using keywords (more on Title and Description meta tags in chapter 6). What about your image "Alt" tags?

_____

_____

_____

_____

6. Are keywords (separated by underscores) used in the naming of your various "internal" webpages? (the part after the " .com/ "

_____

_____

_____

_____

Chapter 4

Incoming Links to Your Site "Backlinks"

Relevant incoming hyperlinks from other sites within your industry (with similar topics as your site) as mentioned earlier, are a high priority. Experts say it's the highest priority with Google.

Getting online editors from your industry trade publications to write a story about your business and put a link to your website is a great way to increase incoming links (backlinks).

Doing a Press Release

A real press release, not an advertisement, based around a newsworthy event is a great way to get editors to do a story on you. You will increase your likelihood of the editor picking up your press release if it is newsworthy to **their** readers. Editors will usually link back to your website from the story they post on their websites.

Tip: One of my best press releases coincided with JetBlue's® inaugural "in-flight internet" flight. I just piggybacked on their historic flight with my press release (making my press release newsworthy) announcing that in-flight internet was the main reason I invented the Aviator Laptop Stand. Many editors asked for review samples to do stories, and they linked the story to my website. A link from the New York Times can do wonders for your ranking.

A wonderful resource for press releases is *www.RapidPressRelease.com*. I have used this press release service for years and I highly recommend them for their awesome customer service, effectiveness, and fair price.

Writing an Article

An article can establish your authority in your area of expertise. Usually, websites who will "post" your article on their website will also provide a link back to your website as the originator of the article. You in turn will want to link to the article from your website. This establishes your creditability with your visitors. It's a win-win for increasing backlinks.

There are hundreds of article submission sites and you might have success with one of them like ***http://ezinearticles.com*** and ***www.goarticles.com***. However, you should focus your article on the leaders and trade publications within your industry. Just contact them directly.

Your article must have enough impact and interest to grab their attention and be of interest to their readers.

Here's an example from my concrete countertop business. I knew I had to get the attention of the editor of our industry's main trade publication with something powerful. Knowing that she is always looking for techniques to share with her readers, I decided to give up one of my "trade secrets" to get her attention. The article proved intersting to her readers because it contained an unusual technique that no one had used before. The article was posted along with the link to my website. Immediately, my ranking went through the roof! I will trade one small "trade secret" for immediate high ranking any day. Plus, six months later, they published the article in their print publication – a double whammy!

> **Tip:** Google has a one-stop-shop where you can submit all kinds of elements and media from your website like press releases, articles, images, and products for sale:
>
> ### *http://base.google.com/base*

Monthly Newsletter

Newsletters not only keep your regular customers coming back for more, they can also increase your back links – if you allow others to post your newsletters on their websites. Giving them permission to do so is a really good idea, but be sure to always request that they recognize the source of the article with a link back to your website.

My other sister is a respiratory therapist and works for a doctor's office specializing in sleep disorders. I was discussing this book with her and she commented that the office manager was complaining that the practice was not receiving that many new (nor younger) patients and wanted to improve their website. I told my sister about fresh content and back links. She said "..but not that much changes around our office to constantly update the website with." Bingo! I suggested that the doctor create a monthly newsletter on current events within the sleep disorder field.

I also suggested that they look for articles already published and available for use or purchase from their industry trade publications or associations. Having a copyrighted article on your website is another great way to increase backlinks. Allow other websites to refer to the articles on your website (by linking to your website). This relieves them of having to pay royalties and fees themselves. We'll see how my suggestion pans out for the doctor's office - in the next edition of this book.

Tip: It is best to ask anyone that is linking to your website to make the hyperlink actual keyword text on their website. In other words, they should not just list your web address as the hyperlink on their site. For example, a good link for me would be the text "Ergonomic Laptop Stands" with this text being an actual hyperlink to my site, versus just making my web address (***www.keynamics.com***) the link. But, any link to your site will help, as long as it does not come from one of those link sharing farms. Beggars can't be choosy.

Google places the highest priority on incoming links. I guess they figure that the more relevant websites that link to your website, the more important you must be. The more popular a website is that links to you, the better – as long as it's relevant.

Site Maps

Although not directly related to this chapter on incoming links, site maps do contain all the links within your own site.

Google will tell you "outright" that having a sitemap on your website helps their search engine spiders index your site easier.

Visit:

https://www.google.com/webmasters/tools/docs/en/ protocol.html or ***http://www.sitemaps.org/*** for sitemap protocol.

Define: Site Map – A page on a website that shows all of the links to all of the other pages within the website. Like a map, it quickly and easily shows a user how to navigate the entire website.

Tip: Check the backlinks to your website by entering:

"link: yourname.com" into the search box on Yahoo or Google. Inserting your actual web address with a space after the colon and omitting quotes.

Tip: Do you visit blogs or discussion forums to post comments, give expert advice or answer technical questions? Be sure to link back to your website (for further details) when doing so.

Social Network Services like *www.myspace.com*, *www.classmates.com* and *www.linkedin.com* are great for backlinks and/or traffic as well. For a list of SNS sites visit:

http://en.wikipedia.org/wiki/List_of_social_networking_ websites

---

Chapter Action Steps / Notes

1. What valuable insight do you have within your industry, which you could share?

_____

_____

_____

_____

2. Ongoing plan for writing newsworthy Press Releases, Articles and Newsletters.

_____

_____

_____

_____

3. Create a site map.

_____

_____

_____

_____

4. Check your backlinks with Google and Yahoo.

_____

_____

Chapter 5

Content is King

Search engines favor websites that have more text than pictures. They also tend to favor websites with more individual webpages of content/text over those with fewer pages. It's important that the text be kept fresh and updated (or at least changed) on a regular basis. Remember that search engines reward websites that are frequently updated with fresh content (see chapter 4 – for ideas on fresh content).

Let's compare updating your website to one of those changeable marquees on the outside of a "brick and mortar" business. Imagine if the owner left the same message on the sign all year. People would just drive by without paying attention to it. Nobody likes a "stale" message.

We had those changeable message boards on our family owned Ace Hardware stores. Growing up, my Dad was adamant about me getting up on that ladder every week to change the letters, so people would pay attention to our messages/advertisements as they drove by. The same goes for your website content. Keep it fresh. (Thanks Dad)

First Two Sentences

It is important to work your keywords into all of your body text within your webpages, but it is paramount that the very first sentence or two, in your *visible text* (in the body of every page) contains all of your keywords. However, this can be tricky, because the text that "appears" to be first on your "visible by humans" web page, might not be what the spiders see first.

To see what the spiders see first, go to your source code (View – Source, up on the top of the Microsoft® Internet Explorer® toolbar) and look for the first appearance of text. To find it, look just after the keyword and description meta tags. There is a <Body> tag.

The sentence you are looking for comes right after this <Body> tag. There might be some image files before the actual text, but you will recognize the text because it will match your visible website text. If your first sentence on your "visible" web page is not physically located here in your code, move it there. Moving the text, along with the programming that surrounds the text, has no bearing on how it appears on the "visible" website – if it is done correctly. The programming "tags" place the text in the proper physical location on your webpage. Remember to back up your program first!

This might be one of the most complicated and important things I discuss in this book. So, you need to figure out how to do it in your website design program or have your programmer do it for you.

Define: Tag – a tag is a small of a piece of programming code (some people call it a "snippet"). You can recognize them by the appearance of the "less than" and "greater than" signs < ABC > in your web design programming code.

Tip: It's paramount to save back up copies of your website, before you make any changes, so you can always revert to the latest revision, in case something goes wrong with the last change you made.

You also need lots of relevant text in the body of every page. When coming up with text, keywords, and file names, think of what people might be searching for when they look for a business like yours. Ask your customers what they might search for when looking up this information. Try searching for those words yourself to see which sites are ranked high.

Then go in and look at the code of your competitors with high ranking (view – source up on the top of the Microsoft®

Internet Explorer® bar). See what their meta tag descriptions and keywords are.

Most importantly, you should show up number one on any search engine when someone types in your actual business name. Insert your business name in a lot of places, but don't overdo it.

Tip: If you're after local customers, you would want to show up high when people search for a particular keyword and the actual name of your city. Therefore, put your city name in as many places as you can, like meta tags, the body text, and file names.

Tip: Earlier I discussed the difference between real text and pictures of text. If you are using a business logo with your name on it, just know that the search engine spiders are *not* going to be able to read the text (i.e. business name) off your picture logo.

Note that Google employs something called LSI (Latent Semantic Indexing). In simple terms it just means that they don't look at the number of times a keyword is repeated on a page; they look at how the keyword is associated with the "theme" or context of the page. Pages written with good text that is relevant to the keywords are best

Chapter Action Steps / Notes

1. Where does your first sentence of text show up in your programming code? Does it contain your most important keywords?

_____

_____

_____

_____

2. Ask customers what they would search for to find your business – especially new ones.

_____

_____

_____

_____

3. Does your copy make sense grammatically, or have you just stuffed a bunch of keywords in?

_____

_____

_____

_____

4. Do you want local customers? Be sure your city or area name is included in your keyword strategy.

_____

_____

_____

_____

5. What's your ongoing strategy for updating with fresh content?

_____

_____

_____

_____

Part II:

Optimizing Websites For Customer Service Helps Google Ranking

Websites designed with music, flashing lights, bells and whistles are just one more barrier between your customer and you making a sale. Sometimes these flashy things are just a way for website designers to show off their programming skills.

Customers have come to the internet (and hopefully to your website) to find the information they need and they want it fast.

Chapter 6

Great! You Have High Ranking – Now What Do You Do?

Well, you want the searching public to pick *you* out of the top ten websites that are displayed on the first page in front of them. The more you are picked, the higher you will be ranked. Self fulfilling!

Google keeps track of how often browsers pick you for any particular keyword search over other websites listed on the first page of search results. Google then rewards those picked more often with higher ranking. I guess they figure that if more people are picking you, your website must be more "relevant" to the searchers keyword.

How to Get Picked From the Results Page

Make sure that your Home page has an attention-grabbing *"Title"* meta tag. Your website design program will have a way to insert a title for each page of your website. Every webpage should have a different title, and the title should contain your most important keyword "phrase" for that particular page.

The title of a webpage is the very first line that shows up *in bold* on each of the ten websites displayed on the Google search engine results page. This is the most visible line of text! The title also shows up on the very top line in your browser window (in the blue bar on Microsoft® Internet Explorer®). You only get a few words and Google truncates the rest, so play around with it.

Think of this Title meta tag as your "**ATTENTION GRABBING HEADLINE**" of a newspaper story. Make sure it has **IMPACT!**

The very next line or two under the bold "Title", on the Google search results is usually the same as the *"Description"* meta tag sentence. Again, make sure it's something that will make the searcher want to click on your link.

The HOOK: Think of this second sentence as your "Call To Action" to reel the browsers in.

On my title, my laptop stand price point of $19.99 is a good attention grabber. (And yes you can put a $ sign and numbers in your title. Just don't try to insert these symbols in your file names.)

Tip: Don't forget to be sure your Title Meta Tag and your Description Meta Tag have your most important keywords in them as well. You have to balance: "The Impact", "the Hook" and "the keywords" all in a couple of sentences!

Tip: Google tracks how many times your website is clicked from the search results page, and this factors into their ranking efforts. So, make sure your site stands out from all the rest, because the more people that click on yours, the higher your rank.

Chapter Action Steps / Notes

1. Title meta tag = your Headline.

_____

_____

_____

_____

2. Description meta tag = your "Call to Action".

_____

_____

_____

_____

3. What titles and descriptions are your competitors using?

_____

_____

_____

_____

Chapter 7

Then Once They Get to Your Website

People searching (paying customers) want information and they want it fast. They don't want to have to wade through a lot of animations, flashing things, or corny music to get it. The ultimate goal? To convert them into paying customers, supporters, or believers in your worthwhile cause.

Define: Conversion Rate — The percentage of customers who you actually "convert" to a paying customer versus the total number of visitors. Usually calculated over a certain period of time.

You want to get the visitor to hang around your site, and come back for a visit on a regular basis. This is called "Stickiness" and Google rewards for stickiness.

Define: Stickiness — The longer customers stay on your website and the more often they come back to visit, the more "Sticky" your site is.

This is not rocket science here. Design your website so it's easy to read, uncluttered, and has a lot of white space (advice that is sometimes hard to follow — it seems like we just want to shout out our message by cramming in bunch of words). Simple really is better.

Tip: Sans Serif fonts (fonts without serifs) are easier to read on computer monitors. A couple of examples are Arial ® and Verdana ®. (Arial is used in all of these text boxes.)

Serifs are non-structural details on the ends of some of the strokes that make up letters and symbols. For example, Times New Roman ® is a serif font. Fonts with serifs, while easier to read in print, are harder to read on computer monitors.

Use Arial ® for type points 12 and above, and Verdana ® for 10 point and below.

The Microsoft® Corporation actually developed the Verdana® font because of the need for a readable font on the early computer monitors. These early monitors had low resolutions making the text look fuzzy. While today's monitors have higher resolutions and are clearer, the Verdana ® font's readability still helps with smaller fonts 10 point and below.

The text in Verdana ® is purposely spaced a little further apart, therefore, on 12 point and higher, it looks too spaced out - like this last sentence.

Tip: Search engines track how long a visitor stays on your website and reward those who's websites are stickier. So keep them longer with intersting and useful content.

Tip: (Worth Repeating) – Never have a "Splash" page.

You might have seen these before. It's like an "introductory" page that a user comes to after typing in the web address. This page plays video, Adobe® Flash® Player, music, or a combination of all three. There is usually a link that reads "Skip Intro" allowing the user to bypass the video and go to the "real" website.

At the end of the video it has on option to enter the "real" website - "Click here to Enter Site".

Always have people land on your ***real*** "home" page, or a specific product page, when they link to, or type in your website address. Splash Pages will hurt your ranking and they are a real pain for users.

Remember, customers want information and they want it fast. Don't place barriers like this between your customer and a purchase decision.

Chapter Action Steps / Notes

1. As soon as the customer lands on your webpage, does it convey the message of the keyword they typed into the search box?

_____

_____

_____

_____

2. Is the landing page cluttered with a bunch of "flashy" stuff?

_____

_____

_____

3. Is your text easy to read?

_____

_____

_____

_____

Chapter 8

Generally Accepted Good Business Practices for Internet Retailing

A positive user experience can improve your ranking as well. It has the potential to increase your incoming links – people like referring a positive experience and might reward you with a link to your site.

A wise old website designer once said: "The three most important things to a website visitor are: Trust, Trust , and Trust"

Some of the following tips are a function of the shopping cart service, and are well beyond the scope of most small business owners to incorporate themselves – including me. However, you should be aware of these practices and make sure that your shopping cart and website design incorporates them. Most shopping cart services are purchased "off the shelf". Therefore, knowing what to look for in the service helps you choose a good one.

Define: Shopping Cart – A shopping cart is a "turnkey" third party service that will provide you with "Web Pages" formatted to take the customer's order, and the customer's payment method. Once your customer clicks the "Add to Cart" button, they are actually leaving your website and going to the secure shopping cart website/server, without even knowing it.

The shopping cart service provides the website programming code and a way to relay the customer's credit card (or PayPal) information to your Merchant Account. Your merchant account then transfers the money to your Bank Account. Usually your merchant account will have certain "approved" shopping carts that it works with. A good shopping cart will allow the pages to have the same look and feel as your main website, so the customers feel like they have never actually "left" your site.

Having a third party handle the shopping cart helps relieve you of tremendous liability (ask your attorney). You don't want to store your customers' credit card information and have to worry about someone hacking into your website and stealing it.

"Building Trust"

Feature Testimonials and Product Reviews

What better way to build trust than from other customers and editorial reviews.

Prominently Feature Your Phone Number

and contact information, especially on the checkout page. Customers find this very reassuring.

Get a Toll Free Number

They are fairly inexpensive these days. A good one will only charge you a small base rate and then a per minute charge. Also list your local number (with area code) – it reassures customers that your business is located in the same area they are in. More than one location? – list all the phone numbers.

Include a Physical Address

on your contact us page, not just a Post Office Box.

Include an "About Us" page

linked from your home page.

Tip: Some would rather have customers complete the buying process online without having to take the customers' phone calls. We have noticed on our laptop stand business, that sometimes online shoppers just want to call to be reassured that we are a reputable business. They are also reassured that they can get in touch with a "Live" person if needed. Once we answer the calls, we encourage the customers to go ahead and complete their purchase online. We do offer to gladly take their order by phone, but we note that it's actually more secure online (because on phone orders we have to write down their credit card information, and our shopping cart's secure server does not store that information). Talking to customers in person is an opportunity to up sell them as well.

Reassure them with your Return Policy

Most of your smarter competitors offer a 30 day return policy. Most credit card merchant accounts require you to offer a 30 day return policy. This is a good business practice and you will want to feature it in a prominent location near the "Add to Cart" button and during the checkout process.

Reassure Them About Your Privacy Policy with a Link to it on Every Page

Define: Privacy Policy —a statement or promise by the website owner not to share (or in any way give out) the visitors' private information (like email addresses or phone numbers). It's also good business practice to state that you will not use their information to contact them (without their permission), unless it is for shipment or pertinent product information like a recall.

Tell Them That Your Shopping Cart is on a Secure Server

Even though most every shopping cart is hosted on a secure server, it's reassuring to let them know that once they click "add to cart" and start the checkout process, they will be entering their sensitive information on a secure server.

Define: Secure Server – You can always tell when you are on a "Secure Server" by the website address. The ***HTTP://www.your-name.com*** changes to ***HTTPS://www.your-name.com.*** The "S" in the HTTPS:// designates a secure server. Secure servers are very restrictive and held to very tight security standards, meaning hackers have a difficult time hacking into them and stealing sensitive information like your customers credit card information!

Use Secure Server Certificates from Well Known Companies like VeriSign

> **Tip:** Don't overemphasize the security issue; it could backfire on you. Some folks might not have thought about losing their credit card information to identity thieves and you may scare them off.

Don't Make People Register on Your Site

People are in a hurry and you should be respectful of their time. Let them buy the item and get going. After all, you are not Amazon or eBay®.

Don't Make People Fill out a Form Just to Send You an Email

Don't make customers fill out a form just to email you from your contact page. Give them an email link, like info@keynamics.com. Do you really like filling out those forms yourself when you just want to ask a quick question?

Ensure that the "Flow" of the Checkout is Logical

You don't want customers to get lost or confused, especially when they are trying to give you their money!

Provide High-Quality, Large Images

High speed broadband is so common now, slow loading websites and large images are less and less of an issue than they were before. Furthermore, a good image editing program like Adobe® Photoshop® can reduce the size of a large picture without reducing the quality.

Put Product Images on your Shopping Cart Landing Page

An image of the product they are buying reassures customers that they are ordering the right product. This improves their comfort levels before even starting the actual checkout process.

Define: Shopping Cart Landing Page – The page that visitors go to just after clicking the "Add to Cart" button. This page "holds" all of the items (like a shopping cart) until the shopper is ready to pay or "check out". Customers have the option to pay immediately after adding one single item to the cart, or they can go back to your main website and add many more items to the cart before proceeding to the final checkout and payment.

Allow the customer to "Return to Shopping" after they land on the "Shopping Cart Landing Page"

Most good shopping carts have this feature prominently displayed. It's a great way to increase "Add On" sales.

Increase Sales with Related Items on Main Website Pages and Especially on the Checkout Landing Page

"May we suggest this XYZ, to go with your ABC"

Be careful with this and any other promotions on your website. You don't want to deter customers from their focus on buying what they intended to buy. For example, a "Pop Up" would be a very bad idea anywhere on your website.

Reduce Abandon Carts with Reassurance

At every step or required action (like asking for their email addresses), reassure them about your privacy policy, or reassure them with your return policy, warranty, etc.

Define: Abandon Carts – Abandon carts are unfortunate and very common among internet shoppers. Basically, you've succeeded in getting found from your high ranking, the customer has chosen an item, they start the checkout process in your shopping cart, and then for some reason they just exit your whole website. Some folks are just curious about shipping and getting familiar with your purchase process, possibly to return later to complete the purchase. But most, unfortunately are lost forever.

What a shame, after all of the effort to get them to your site and choose an item - then to lose them.

Display the Shipping Amount / Options on the Checkout Landing Page

Don't make them go half way through the checkout process just to find out the shipping amount, or the methods you offer to ship. Most shopping carts can "estimate" this at the checkout landing page for each type of shipping service you offer.

Don't Make the Customer Repeat Typing Entries

Typically your shopping cart will ask for the "billing" address and the "shipping" address. Many times the two addresses are different, but if they are the same, allow the customer to just check a box that says it's the same. Use this for email addresses as well, if you ask for it more than once.

Place the "Add to Cart" Button in Obvious Places

Don't make it hard for your customers to instantly click and make a purchase. Put the "Add to Cart" button right by the product image. After all, you will have repeat customers who come back to your website, knowing exactly what they want, and wanting to place the order ASAP.

It's also a good practice to have both the item and the "Add to Cart" button visible on the first or "top" screen. The idea is to be "above the fold" and **not** have to scroll down to see this.

Allow People to Easily Go Back to the Previous Page Using the "Back Button" to Correct Mistakes

Some shopping carts lose everything if you hit the back button and the customer has to start all over. Many will just "Abandon" the checkout process all together if this happens.

Put a Search Box on Every Page of your Website

Visitors probably found your site by typing a keyword into a search box. Let them continue the search on your website.

> **Tip:** Google provides a search feature that you can employ on your website. See www.google.com/sitesearch

Your Contact Information, Privacy Policy and Return Policy Should be HIGHLY Visible on the Checkout Landing Page

The trust factor is never more important than at the checkout landing page.

Never Let Customers Actually Leave Your Website When They Click on an External Link (to another website)

This can be accomplished by making sure that these outbound links open a new (and smaller) browser window, thus keeping your website open in the background.

Never *Ever* Disable the "Back Button" on Your Website

This is so annoying, as it looses all of the web visitors' previous website "surfing" history, making them start their search process all over again. You are being held "hostage" on the website. When this happens to me, I vow never to visit that website nor do business with them again! I bet I am not alone.

Tip: Some of the policies and ideas mentioned above might seem so obvious to you or your industry that you don't think they merit featuring on your website. You might be thinking "Everybody knows that".

Just remember – "If you don't show it, people will assume that you don't offer it".

Chapter Action Steps / Notes

How can I build trust on my website?

_____

_____

_____

_____

_____

_____

_____

_____

_____

_____

Personal Note from the Author

A Final Word on your SEO Efforts

My best advice is to start researching articles on the subject of SEO (Search Engine Optimization) because the internet changes daily. I spend about fifteen minutes a day researching and looking over my site to find ways to improve it. A great place to do SEO research is Google's area designed especially for web designers: *http://www.google.com/support/webmasters*

Whether or not you design your website yourself – knowledge is power. Your website represents you and your business to the world and this is way too important to go on blind faith. Would you let a stranger run your cash register or wait on your best customer? Arm yourself with the knowledge contained within this book so you can talk intelligently with a website designer. After all, a good website designer will rely on you for input. To be able to give good input, you must have a basic understanding of SEO.

You can hire out SEO, but there are a lot of amateurs around because anyone can claim to be a website designer or SEO expert – so be careful and be prepared. If you feel that you are up to the task – do it yourself. You know your business best – plus, a web designer would have to be paid each time any little update needs to be implemented on your site. Worse yet, how long would you have to wait for the update to actually happen? Remember, your advantage over large corporations is quick reaction to changes.

If you do hire a website designer, find one that asks you lots of questions about your business – it should be a combined effort. Find one that will show you how to make subtle changes/updates yourself, and only rely on them for major updates.

We will refer reputable website designers on our website. If you are a website designer and you agree with the underlying principles outlined in this book (mainly finding out as much as you can about the customer's business – first and foremost), then please contact us via our website for details on inclusion. You will also want to use this book as a guide to facilitate communication between you and the business owner.

I am available for presentations to groups and would love to speak at your next function, relating the proven strategies within this book – in laymen's terms. Business owner to business owner.

www.get-top-ranking-on-search-engines.com

Good Luck & Thanks for Reading! – Greg Bright

Useful Websites:

Google's advice on SEO and hiring for it:

http://www.google.com/support/webmasters/bin/answer.py?hl=en&answer=35291

Google's advice on Improving Page ranking:

http://www.google.com/support/webmasters/bin/answer.py?answer=34432&ctx=sibling

Registering your URL with Google:

http://www.google.com/addurl/

Registering your business location with Google:

http://www.google.com/local/add/

Find out your competitors' website traffic:

http://www.trafficestimate.com/

For quickly linking to the above pages and more useful links – please see

www.get-top-ranking-on-search-engines.com

Action Plan

In an ideal world, the following steps would be great to implement. However, if you can't start at the beginning (maybe you already have an established business name or website URL), then just pick any topic or tip in this book and get started early.

1. Research keywords and decide on your top three for your home page and also for every other page.

---

2. Study competitors' websites using the tips from page 48 and 52 to find out their strategies.

---

3. Name your business *and* your URL a name with the most important keywords in it.

---

4. Register your free business listing with Google Local Business Center (page 26) if you want local customers.

---

5. Start contacting others within your industry with press releases and articles – and start "fishing" for backlinks (Chapter 4).

_____

_____

_____

6. Don't do anything that will get you banned or penalized (Chapter 2).

_____

_____

_____

7. Make sure every single file in your website is named with a keyword (Chapter 3).

_____

_____

_____

8. Research SEO often.

_____

_____

_____

9. Always keep good customer service in mind when designing your website (Part II).

_____

_____

_____

10. Update – Update – Update your website every week with useful, fresh text and/or new images.

_____

_____

_____

Author's Websites

Greg Bright is an inventor, as well as a small business owner. He received a patent for his ergonomic laptop stand. The Aviator Laptop Stand is praised by the ergonomic community as a solution to the discomforts and health risks associated with hunching over laptops for extended periods of time. The stand weighs just 9 ounces, folds flat to store in the side pocket of a laptop case and is designed for travel and mobility. It is eco-friendly (recycled plastic) and made in the USA.

The Aviator laptop Stand is available at various online retailers, retail stores and direct from the author's website – www.keynamics.com

www.keynamics.com ® – (ergonomic office products)

www.laptop-ergonomics.com – (used to establish authority in computer ergonomics and to backlink to main website)

www.office-chair-ergonomics.com – (used to establish authority in seating ergonomics and to backlink to main website)

www.keyboard-ergonomics.com – (used to establish authority in keyboard ergonomics and to backlink to main website)

www.one-laptop-per-child.com – (searching for grant monies to study the long term affects of laptop usage on young children)

www.islerealty.com – (established in 1997 – For Sale)

www.ancient-art-concrete-countertops.com – (another business)

www.cooler-faster.com – (another invention – For Sale)

Glossary

Abandon Carts – Abandon carts are unfortunate and very common among internet shoppers. Basically, you've succeeded in getting found from your high ranking, the customer has chosen an item, they start the checkout process in your shopping cart, and then for some reason they just exit your whole website. Some folks are just curious about shipping and getting familiar with your purchase process, possibly to return later to complete the purchase. But most, unfortunately are lost forever. What a shame, after all of the effort to get them to your site and choose an item - then to lose them.

Algorithms – The rules that search engines use to rank webpages.

Alt Tags – Alt tags are the little boxes of text that show up when you hold your cursor over any picture on a website. ALT stands for "alternative text" and helps the visually impaired.

Brick and Mortar Business – a brick and mortar business is a business in the traditional sense. It has a physical location, versus an internet business, which might only exist on the web.

Broken Link — A link that does not work. You click on it and you get a blank webpage that says something like "Internet Explorer cannot display the webpage".

Conversion Rate — The percentage of customers who you actually "convert" to a paying customer versus the total number of visitors. Usually calculated over a certain period of time.

Hosting Company — A hosting company actually "hosts" (or stores) your website program files (usually along with other website customers' program files) on a hard drive on their server. Servers allow your website to be accessed by internet users on the world wide web. They usually charge a "rental" fee for this service based on your website size and traffic. This negates the need to have your own server, which would have to be professionally maintained. Some things are wise to rent out.

Hosting Server — The internet is just a bunch of servers connected to each other worldwide. These servers are nothing more than a fancy version of your home personal computer. They are typically stacked on top of one another and the company that ***hosts*** websites might have rows and rows of these "stacks". Your website program will be "hosted" on one of those servers. Most of us rent that space on a "shared" server, meaning that we share the hard drive space (on one of the servers) with many other websites that are hosted on that same server's hard drive.

HTML – (Hypertext Markup Language) The programming language that most websites are written in.

Hyperlink – A hyperlink is any link that opens another page on the internet from your current page, typically designated by the little arrow on your pointer changing to a hand.

Incoming Links – Incoming links are when any other website has created a clickable hyperlink to your website. These are also referred to as "Backlinks". Hyperlink and Link are used interchangeably.

Index – Indexing is just a fancy word meaning that a particular search engine has included your website within its search results. In other words, they have found you.

Keyword – A keyword is any word (or phrase) that a searcher might type into the search box of any search engine.

Keyword Stuffing – Repeating keywords over and over in certain areas of your website – stuffing it full of keywords. This usually penalizes you. For example, you will get penalized if you repeat a bunch of keywords in your keyword meta tag or in the body of your text on any webpage.

Meta Tags – programming code that works in the background of any website, the most common being HTML – Hypertext Markup Language.

Micro Business — Technically, a small business as defined by the SBA has less than $5 million in sales and less than 500 employees. A Micro Business might have zero employees and can be run by one or two people (typically family members). I tend to view a Micro Business and a "Mom and Pop" business as one in the same.

Natural Search Results — Most search engines return about ten individual website results on the first page after a searcher types a keyword into the search box – this is called the Search Engine Results Page – SERP. The individual ten listings are referred to as the "natural" search results. Do not confuse them with the sponsored (paid advertising) links that are usually listed on the right side of the page with a few sometimes listed just above the natural results. These "advertisements" are usually indicated as "Paid" or "Sponsored" ads. Natural search results are free.

Privacy Policy — a statement or promise by the website owner not to share (or in any way give out) the visitors' private information (like email addresses or phone numbers). It's also good business practice to state that you will not use their information to contact them (without their permission), unless it is for shipment or pertinent product information like a recall.

Secure Server – You can always tell when you are on a "Secure Server" by the website address. The ***HTTP://www.your-name.com*** changes to ***HTTPS://www.your-name.com***. The "S" in the HTTPS:// designates a secure server. Secure servers are very restrictive and held to very tight security standards, meaning hackers have a difficult time hacking into them and stealing sensitive information like your customers credit card information!

SEO – SEO stands for "Search Engine Optimization" and involves designing your website to be search-engine-friendly with the goal of high ranking – so your website can be found on the internet through search engines.

Shopping Cart – A shopping cart is a "turnkey" third party service that will provide you with "Web Pages" formatted to take the customer's order, and the customer's payment method. Once your customer clicks the "Add to Cart" button, they are actually leaving your website and going to the secure shopping cart website/server, without even knowing it.

Shopping Cart Landing Page – The page that visitors go to just after clicking the "Add to Cart" button. This page "holds" all of the items (like a shopping cart) until the shopper is ready to pay or "check out". Customers have the option to pay immediately after adding one single item to the cart, or they can go back to your main website and add many more items to the cart before proceeding to the final checkout and payment.

Site Map – A page on a website that shows all of the links to all of the other pages within the website. Like a map, it quickly and easily shows a user how to navigate the entire website.

Spider – Search engines have programs (called Spiders or "Bots") that go out and look at every single website on the internet. They "crawl" every aspect (including file names, text and the actual programming code), of every page of every website on the internet attempting to rank them by subject matter. They rank both the home page and the individual pages – mostly relating them to keywords that searchers might enter into the search box of the search engine. Again, the page being ranked could be the "Home Page" (the home page is the most important) or any other page within the website.

Splash Page – These are pages that usually have some sort of fancy video, music or Adobe® Flash® Player animation that visitors must sit through first, before they can "Click to Enter" the main "Real" website.

Stickiness – The longer customers stay on your website and the more often they come back to visit, the more "Sticky" your site is.

Tag – a tag is a small of a piece of programming code (some people call it a "snippet"). You can recognize them by the appearance of the "less than" and "greater than" signs < ABC > in your web design programming code.

Text Link – A link (or hyperlink) is simply a way to jump from one webpage to another, whether it's within the various pages of your site or linking outside to another website. A link is typically designated by the arrow on your pointer changing to a hand once placed over the link. The link can be a picture (or image) or it can be actual text. If it's text it can be composed of keywords, or it can be the actual web address of the page it's going to. Using "text" links, composed of your important keywords is the **only** way to go. You can always tell if it's a text link by being able to highlight the actual text (for example if you wanted to copy and paste the text). You can't highlight text from a picture link – because there is not any text there. Also, text links are usually underlined and usually change color when your mouse pointer runs over them.

URL – URL stands for **U**niform **R**esource **L**ocator and is the part of the web address between the www. and the .com It's the address that people find you by when pulling up your website on the internet, also known as the domain name.

Breinigsville, PA USA
13 January 2011
253279BV00004B/9/P